Siskins &
Goldfinches

Peter Lander and Bob Partridge

Photographer: Dennis Avon MIOP A.R.P.S.

Siskins & Goldfinches

Peter Lander and Bob Partridge

KINGDOM

Published by Kingdom Books
PO Box 15
Waterlooville PO7 6BQ
England

Contents

Preface

This book is the second in a series intended as a follow-on to the very successful book *British Birds in Aviculture*, published in conjunction with the British Bird Council. By concentrating on no more than three species in each book we can treat them in much greater depth. It also enables us to update the original book where necessary in the light of the latest knowledge and experience.

Our old friend the late Walter Lewis always used to say, 'The golden rule in bird breeding is that there is no golden rule.' By this he meant that there are always exceptions in anything to do with birds, and the experience of one successful breeder is totally different from that of another, for no apparent reason. Walter was considered to be one of the most knowledgeable British fanciers of his time in the field of British birds, mules and hybrids.

All we can do is pass on our knowledge and experience as a basis on which each breeder can develop his or her own system. As joint authors we can sometimes give different information, hopefully making this book all the more interesting and useful.

Peter Lander and Bob Partridge

Popular British Birds in Aviculture:

No 1: Greenfinches   *No 2: Siskins and Goldfinches*

No 3: Redpolls, Twites and Linnets   *No 4: Bullfinches, Chaffinches and Bramblings*

<u>Cages and Aviaries</u>

Before obtaining any birds it is essential to have suitable accommodation. While this need be neither expensive nor ornamental, it must be suitable for the birds' needs. They must have room to move about freely, shelter from the elements and protection from enemies such as cats, owls, weasels, rats and other vermin. There must also be sufficient food and water receptacles.

Birds certainly look better in an aviary but, for enthusiasts who have neither the space nor the means, adequate accommodation can be provided in cages. These can be situated in a shed in the garden. However, many sheds need extra windows to allow the birds enough light to feed throughout the day - if the shed is dark they will spend a lot of time roosting. There must be good ventilation, allowing continuous free passage of air. Heating is not necessary for temperate-zone birds normally resident in this country throughout the year. On the other hand, it is essential that the birds can drink at all times during the day and, unless the fancier is at home all day, the shed should be heated or insulated sufficiently to prevent the water from freezing during severe weather. A study of the advertisements in the fancy press will produce information on sheds in a variety of shapes and sizes, all designed for bird keeping.

Birds need room if they are to breed - in fact the larger the cage the better. The minimum size recommended is 91cm (36in) long by 60cm (24in) high by 46cm (18in) back to front, containing only one pair. Far better results will be obtained by having a few pairs in large cages than by having more pairs in smaller cages. Natural branches can be fixed in the cages for perches; these look nicer and are much more comfortable for the birds' feet than the round doweling often used, but do not overcrowd the cage with these as flying space is essential. In one end of the cage fix a bunch of conifer or other suitable evergreen, with a forked branch in the middle to support a nest. Alternatively a small wicker basket or half-open-fronted, open-topped box can be used (fig 1). The object is to provide privacy and a feeling of security for the sitting hen, but the bunch must not be thick enough to exclude too much light or prevent the birds from entering easily: just enough to give the necessary seclusion.

Contrary to advice frequently given, the most consistent results are obtained in sheds and aviaries facing east. This is because birds, particularly when nesting, do not like being

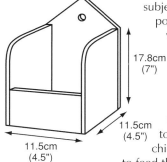

17.8cm
(7")

11.5cm
(4.5")

11.5cm
(4.5")

Fig 1: Nest box

subjected to the mid-day sun and, in the wild, nearly always choose a shaded position. They also like protection from the prevailing west winds and, in the wild, choose a situation that is protected in this respect also. It is not always possible to provide the ideal so it is advisable to fix up some means of providing shade and protection.

The only real disadvantage to cage breeding is the extra work involved in providing a sufficient variety of foods on which the birds can feed their young, particularly when they are first hatched. Even in a small aviary it is much easier to provide a variety of foods, and the birds will find a few insects to supplement their diet, which can be so beneficial in the early stages of a chick's life. To some extent this can be overcome if the birds can be persuaded to feed the young ones on egg food. More details on feeding are given in chapter 5.

It is not essential to provide near-natural conditions to breed our popular native birds. The majority of these common species can be reproduced with the minimum of cover in a small flight. Even a large cage will suffice for many of the hardbills.

Some years ago breeders used large amounts of cover in the form of gorse, broom, conifers and other evergreens but nowadays the birds are much more domesticated and breed very successfully with only a minimum of cover. This has the added benefit of allowing the breeder to observe, study and enjoy the birds to a far greater degree.

Aviary Construction

An aviary can be any size but the minimum recommended is 180cm (6ft) long by 60cm (2ft) wide by 180cm (6ft) high. This will hold approximately six non-breeding birds, but generally only one pair of breeding birds. In a mixed aviary one should allow at least 2.25 cubic metres (80 cubic feet) per pair of birds; much more if possible.

Aviaries can be as simple or as elaborate as one wishes, depending on circumstances and funds available, as long as they meet the requirements of the birds. An example of a cheap and easily-constructed aviary is the one designed some years ago by Mr Hylton Blythe (figure 2), which is made as follows. Roofing laths are driven into the ground at 1m (3ft) intervals and cut off to the required height, with further laths nailed along the top and across from side to side. This enables 1m (3ft) wire netting to be stapled to the laths. There is a small door at one end for access, with a shelf above it for food. A further small door gives access to the shelf so that it is not necessary to enter the aviary to feed the birds. Cover must be provided to keep the seed and shelf dry. The birds also need protection from the wind and rain and shade from the sun. This can be achieved by nailing boards all round along the top to a width of about 30cm (12in) and the same along the top of the sides. Roofing felt can be used instead of boards if there is wire netting under-

Yellow dark goldfinch mule cock (see chapter 9)

neath to support it. If all the timber is treated with creosote or bitumen it will last much longer.

Where funds allow, more substantial aviaries can give added protection to the birds and last considerably longer. A well-constructed and well-maintained aviary can more than repay the extra expense and labour. For example, solid foundation plinths set well into the ground constructed of 10cm (4in) bricks, blocks or solid concrete 45cm (14in) deep will keep out rats. The base area can then be filled in with earth, pebbles,

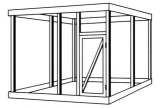

Fig 2: Typical Aviary – from an original design by Hylton Blythe

sand, bark chippings or solid concrete or slabs for easy cleaning and disinfecting. Tanalised framing or cedar wood 50mm x 50mm (2in x 2in) will last almost a life time.

Solid timber felted roofs give valuable protection from cats, kestrels, marauding magpies and thunderstorms and also exclude droppings from wild birds, which can pass on disease to the aviary inmates. Solid cladding of the back and at least one third of the sides gives added protection as well as security to the birds (fig 3 and 4).

Large feeding trays can be provided in a completely dry area where they are clear of any perches, thus preventing the birds from eating mouldy or soiled foods. These and many other refinements can be considered for the welfare of the birds, which is paramount if success is to be achieved.

For nesting sites, use small wickerwork baskets with a few twigs tacked around. This gives the birds some degree of privacy. Even so, many birds pick nesting sites completely open to view, despite other more secluded sites being available. Two or three sites should be available to each pair of birds. Provide a little extra cover for any particularly shy specimens. Other acceptable nesting sites are square wooden pans with perforated

South American black-chinned siskin cock (see chapter 2)

zinc bottoms. These are used by many breeders of canaries. Canary plastic pans will need to have felt linings glued or sewn inside, but the birds often pull these to pieces, leaving the slippery plastic surface on which they cannot shape a nest. However, a little polyfilla or plaster of Paris wiped roughly around the inside can be helpful. Plywood or cane strawberry punnets or clay flower pots can also be used. Sites and receptacles will depend on what the birds find acceptable.

Any simple structure with suitably-sized netting will keep birds in, but it is much more difficult to keep vermin out. Some refinements have already been mentioned to overcome this but, if you do not intend to have solid plinths and solid roofs, other methods have to be used. Cats can be a nuisance, especially if they get on the top of an aviary. To overcome this the main frame should be extended about 23cm (9in) and this extension covered with 5cm (2in) netting, often called chicken wire. Cats have difficulty in walking on this netting, and bunches of gorse hung facing downwards on the corner posts will deter them from climbing up.

Rats, if they gain access, will kill the birds and drag them down their holes, so that they all suddenly disappear. This can be overcome by digging a trench round the aviary 30cm (12in) deep and 30cm (12in) wide. The wire netting is extended down the side of the trench and along the bottom in the shape of a letter L. The trench is then filled in.

Mice are much more difficult to exclude. Although they do not kill birds directly, they carry diseases and cause considerable disturbance, jeopardising breeding results. Also, where mice can get in, weasels will follow and they kill and eat every bird in sight in no time at all. Mice and weasels can get through 1.30cm (1/2in) netting which is generally used for aviaries: 1cm (0.375in) netting, which is much more expensive, will keep out all but baby mice. It is therefore very important to keep a sharp look out and take quick action if any signs of mice are seen by setting traps

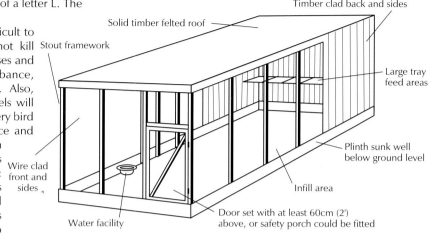

Fig 3: A well constructed aviary 1.8m x 3.6m x 1.8m (6ft x 12ft x 6ft) would accommodate 4 mixed pairs or up to 20 non-breeding birds

and putting down poison. Both traps and poison must be suitably protected from pets and children, especially as they generally cannot be placed inside the aviary. There are now, however, some traps which catch the mice alive and which can be used inside an aviary safely.

A small aviary for each pair of birds is considered ideal, especially if it is your intention to specialise in a particular species. On the other hand, large aviaries containing several species, such as pairs of redpolls, siskins, linnets, twites and goldfinches, will prove perfectly satisfactory. Greenfinches can usually be trusted with these smaller finches throughout the year, and can also be housed with finches of their own size, such as bullfinches, chaffinches, bramblings or buntings, outside the breeding season, though it is not recommended that these species are mixed during the breeding season. Housing of all species needs careful consideration to suit individual needs.

Trouble can be experienced when just two pairs of different species are kept and bred in one aviary, because one pair will sometimes chase the other continually, preventing feeding. It is best to have either one pair or three or more pairs in a flight. This usually prevents the trouble, but always provide a large feeding area or several smaller ones.

The pros and cons of different materials for the floor area, touched on earlier, are really governed by the condi-

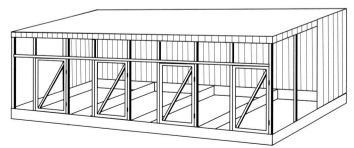

Fig 4: A similar sized aviary partitioned to take 4 segregated breeding pairs; a front corridor could be added for safety

Isolated Type of Nesting Site

a: Basket wired to
stout twigs

b: Surrounded by evergreen
twigs and wire-tied

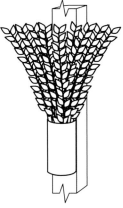

c: Finished nesting site
inserted in down-pipe
which has been fixed
to framework

Fig 5: Nesting sites

tions and needs of both the birds and the keeper. Earth is the natural floor covering and, provided that overstocking is avoided, the birds can derive much benefit in the form of trace elements from the soil. Waste seeds which germinate are a welcome addition to the birds' diet. The vegetation attracts myriad insect life, which again is very beneficial, especially when young are being reared. The drawback is that it is difficult to prevent mice from burrowing in and breeding in the aviary, contaminating both the food and the soil. Earth floors are also difficult to disinfect and keep clean. Liming annually will help to keep it sweet, but the soil will undoubtedly need renewing completely to a depth of 15cm (6in) every few years if problems with disease are to be avoided. Small washed pebbles laid to a depth of 10-15cm (4-6in) are a good alternative. Seeds will still germinate and the birds derive benefit from searching amongst the pebbles. Mice will not take up residence if a good depth of loose pebbles is maintained. Pebbles can easily be riddled to remove waste, washed and disinfected.

Forest bark chippings on an earth floor can look very attractive and again discourage mice if a good covering is maintained. The bark should be about 8-10cm (3-4in) deep and will need to be raked over now and again to freshen it up. It will also need to be removed and replenished from time to time. The spent bark can be composted and used in the garden.

Concrete is sterile and stark and can be cold and damp during inclement weather, but the dampness can be almost eliminated by laying plastic sheeting down before concreting. A layer of sand on top of the finished floor will take away the starkness. It has the advantage of being easy to clean and disinfect and is rodent-proof.

Solid wood floors are also worth considering, having similar benefits to concrete, but being much warmer. However, this type of floor will need to be raised some 30cm (12in) above the ground, allowing a good air flow beneath it to prevent rotting and stopping rodents from gaining access. The whole structure can be set on stilts such as concrete pillars or blocks and bricks with plenty of ventilation holes.

We now come to furnishing the aviary. Most hardbills (and siskins and goldfinches are no exceptions) quickly defoliate any living plants and shrubs. Most will not survive such treatment for long, although vegetation such as elderberry, blackberry and stinging nettles sometimes survives if the aviary is not over-populated. The aviary should be furnished with natural branches such as willow, ash, elder, hazel, apple or pear. These should be located sparsely and high up, providing safe perching and roosting places but still leaving plenty of space for flying exercise.

Since growing shrubs are not usually practical when you are keeping hardbills, substitutes must be provided. There are various ways of doing this using evergreen branches from the conifer tree family. Where single pairs are housed a couple of isolated nesting sites will be found adequate. These are made by wiring a few short branches or twigs of the chosen evergreen around a wickerwork basket or some other similar receptacle (fig 5). For most birds these should be fixed fairly high, close to the roof. Short lengths of gutter down-pipe (approximately 15cm (6in) of 6.5cm (2.5 in) diameter) screwed to the framework in suitable places can easily be fixed and replaced as required. Where several pairs are housed together at least two such sites must be provided for each pair. They can also be made a little more substantial to give each pair rather more privacy. This will prove helpful in avoiding the odd skirmish of pairs guarding territory.

Many breeders find the hedge system by far the most satisfactory. Strange to say, a continuous hedge all down one side or the back seems to overcome territorial problems, and pairs nest close to each other without any fighting. The artificial hedge is built in the following way. Vertical spacers about 5cm (2in) thick are fastened to the side of the aviary. Then laths are nailed horizontally about 25cm (10in) apart, starting from the top. It is not necessary to go below about 75cm (30in) from the floor. If possible, choose the west or south-west side. If the outside of this part of the aviary is of wood, or some other solid material, so much the better. If not, cover it with hessian or roofing felt to provide protection and privacy. Bare, forked branches are now placed in the laths to simulate the inside of a hedge.

After this, conifer branches or other evergreens such as heather and gorse are threaded into the laths producing a finish rather like an uncut hedge. It is important that this should not be too thick and that there are holes in the foliage through which the birds can obtain access to the inside of the hedge where they will build their nests. Do not forget to put a covering 30–46cm (12–18in) wide on the outside of the aviary over the top of the hedge to provide shade from the sun and shelter from the rain.

If birds are to be kept in a very open aviary all the year round, it is best to attach some sort of shelter shed to it so that the feeding can take place inside, and it may be necessary on occasions to confine the birds inside as well. The shelter shed can be as large or small as you desire, or it can be the main bird room with the aviary built on the side. A container full of grit and a bath of fresh water are other essentials to the aviary.

If the birds are being bred in cages in a shed it is very helpful to have a small flight built on to the end of the shed. The birds are fed inside the shed with a pop-hole to give access to the flight. Young birds, when fully weaned, can be transferred to this flight, leaving the parents free to get on with the next nest. Most birds moult out better in a flight where they have access to fresh air with plenty of exercise and bathing facilities.

It is recommended that all birds be ringed, and it is worth bearing this point in mind when deciding on the feeding stations. For some pairs it is a great help if the feeding stations can be somewhat obscured from the nesting sites, making it easier for you to ring the chicks unobserved while the parents feed.

As previously mentioned, aviaries can be as large or small, as ornamental or heavily-built, as the owner wishes, but all will follow the basic pattern of design described and illustrated in the sketches. Refinements can be added according to individual taste.

One point that should be stressed is that it is better not to have the doors too large unless a safety porch is included. If doors are made 90–120cm (3–4ft) high and approximately 60cm (2ft) wide, an area of 60–90cm (2–3ft) will be left above the door on the usual 2m (6ft) aviary. Birds flying towards the door will go to this space above it as you approach and enter, reducing the possibility of escape. The door should be set well clear of the ground so that it opens and closes freely. Doors can open inwards or outwards to suit the needs of the keeper.

Rambler roses, honeysuckle, clematis, hop and other climbing plants can be grown up the outside of the aviary. They look very attractive and help to attract greenfly and other insects from which the birds will benefit. However, the growth must not be allowed to interfere with the general maintenance of the aviary. If the growth should penetrate the wire netting for a prolonged period it can soon create holes that are large enough to allow birds to escape. This can easily happen before the damage is noticed by the keeper.

White campion

Evolution

According to geologists, South Africa and South America were one land mass millions of years ago. We are also told that there were several ice ages within this period, during which most of Europe and North America would have been covered in ice. Neither our European birds nor their North American counterparts could have survived where they were under those conditions, so they moved southwards into the African/South American land mass, joining the populations that were already resident there. This explains why we find striking similarities between some species of Eurasian/African and American birds that otherwise would be inexplicable.

The canary *(Serinus canarius)* is a mutated form of the serin *(Serinus serinus)*. The greenfinch *(Carduelis chloris)* has also evolved from the serin and is therefore closely related.

Another very closely related bird is the siskin *(Carduelis spinus)*. This is proved by the fact that the red factor canary has been produced from fertile hybrids between another closely related species, the red-hooded siskin *(Carduelis cucullata)*, and the canary. Also there have been authenticated breedings between a siskin mule (siskin x canary hybrid) and a canary hen, showing that a percentage of these F1 hybrids are fertile.

Since there are siskins in South America and South Africa, the species clearly evolved long ago, before the geological split beween the two countries. There are no less than 14 members of the genus Serinus in South Africa, including 12 species of canary and two of siskin, all varying geographically. The siskins and five of the species of canary are yellow-ground birds, while the seven remaining species of canary are white-ground birds. As we shall see later, a number of our European species have lost the yellow ground colour.

In South America there are eight species of siskin. Among these are the black siskin *(Carduelis strata)*, which is black all over except for goldfinch-like wing bars and a yellow area under the tail, the black-headed and hooded siskins and, finally, the black-chinned siskin *(Carduelis barbata)*, which is very similar to our European siskin except for the wing and flank markings. There is also the lesser goldfinch *(Carduelis psaltria)*, which looks like a siskin without the black cap and chin but has white tips to its flight feathers reminiscent of, but not exactly like, the goldfinch. All of these are confined to particular areas of the country by mountains and other geological features.

Pair of hooded red siskins (cock: left, hen: right)

Grey-headed eastern goldfinch cock

In North America there are four species:
- The pine siskin *(Carduelis pinus)*: similar to our siskin, but browner and without the black cap and bib.
- The lesser goldfinch (described above), and also a black-backed variation of this with black back, wings and head.
- The American goldfinch *(Carduelis tristis)*: the cock has a black forehead, wings and tail and a yellow body.
- Lawrence's goldfinch *(Carduelis lawrencei)*: again the cock has a black face or blaze, and its upper parts are mostly brown with yellow underparts. The wing markings are similar to both the European siskin and goldfinch.

Of these four species only the pine siskin and the American goldfinch breed right across North America, the other two being confined to small areas along the western coast. It can be seen that, if these species were found in Europe, they might be classed as intermediate forms between the siskin and goldfinch. However, if there were any intermediate forms in Europe they must have died out a long time ago.

There appears to be a gap between birds in South Africa and our European siskin, which is a northern bird confined mainly to areas where birch trees, pine and conifers grow. This also suggests that intermediate species might have been lost, possibly during the ice ages. There is, however, an intermediate species between the greenfinch and the siskin: the Himalayan or black-headed greenfinch *(Carduelis spinoides)* is found in the Himalayas, Northern India and Pakistan and has the beak, head and body of the greenfinch but markings more similar to the siskin, including the black cap. It is possible that the European and American birds have evolved separately, but the similarities are quite remarkable. In any case, the fact that birds from both continents have produced fertile hybrids with the canary proves beyond doubt that they are all closely related.

Up until now we have been dealing with birds with a yellow ground colour. However, the goldfinch *(Carduelis carduelis)* has lost the yellow except in the wing bars and blaze (which is based on yellow) and is basically a white-ground bird. The red in the blaze is conditioned by its food. This is shown by the fact that, when fed incorrectly, the goldfinch moults out with a yellowish blaze that is retained until the bird moults again.

Coltsfoot

There is a link between the greenfinch and the goldfinch: the Chinese or oriental greenfinch *(Carduelis sinica)*, originating in Central and Eastern China. This bird, which has the head, beak and body of the greenfinch with the wing and tail markings of the goldfinch, has produced fertile hybrids with the greenfinch.

Another intermediate form is the grey-headed goldfinch *(Carduelis caniceps)*. This has a grey-brown head, lacking the black head of the European goldfinch but retaining the red blaze. The grey-headed goldfinch is predominantly a mountain bird, found on the forest edge from the north of the Himalayas into Siberia and to the south-east of the Caspian Sea. Where the two species overlap they interbreed, apparently producing young with similarities of both forms. The black-headed European goldfinch lives mainly in lowland parks, gardens and agricultural areas.

Chapter 2

Charlock

Only in recent years has it been realised how important a part imprinting plays in the lives of birds. It has now been shown that hybrids, when mating, show a distinct preference for the species of the hen that reared them. This may explain why hybrids were previously considered to be sterile and it may well account for the evolution of certain species.

There is no similar bird to the goldfinch in Africa other than in the north-west area, where the European bird also breeds. In America the so-called American goldfinch is much more like the siskin. It would seem that the goldfinch has evolved in Eurasia and is much more recent than the other species we have been discussing. Nevertheless, all these species are very closely related.

Pair of black siskins (left: cock, right: hen)

Lifestyle in the Wild -
Siskins

Order: Passeriforms
Family: Fringillidae (Finches)
Genus: *Carduelis*
Species: *Carduelis spinus*
Common Name: Siskin

Description
Length: 11cm (4.25in)
Weight: 10g (0.35oz)
Wing Span: 15cm (6in)
Tarsus:1.25 cm (0.5in)

Cock
A small, yellow-green bird with dark streaks on the back and flanks. Paler below. Blackish crown and bib, but the size of the bib varies considerably and it is sometimes absent altogether. Yellow rump and yellow wing bar. Dark forked tail with yellow sides. See photograph on page 23.

Hen
The yellow colouring is much reduced, giving a greyish appearance. More of the bolder dark streaks than the cock, especially on the flanks and into the chest. No black on crown or bib. See photograph on page 20.

Juveniles
Very similar to the hen, with even stronger striping.

Bill
Short, conical and pointed, similar to, but much shorter than, that of the goldfinch, dark brown in colour.

Legs and Feet
Very short legs and comparatively large feet, enabling it to feed upside-down by hanging tit-like on branches and cones. Colour: dark brown.

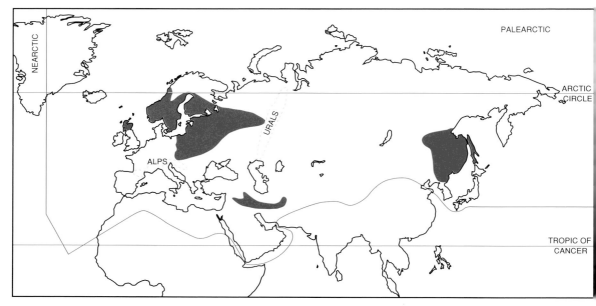

Siskin distribution world-wide

Crop
Siskins have extendable gullets for storing food, either for regurgitation to the hen and youngsters or to help the bird last through the long winter nights.

Distribution
The European siskin is a northern bird confined to pine, larch and fir woods. Its main breeding range extends to most of Northern Europe and part of Russia, up to the tree line south of the Arctic circle. It breeds in Scotland and the central European countries. In winter it is forced south to find food. There is also a breeding population in the far east but, although there is suitable habitat between these two areas, siskins are absent as breeding birds. As with many European species, the northern birds tend to be larger than their southern counterparts.

Habitat
The siskin is dependent upon coniferous and sometimes mixed woods, especially spruce. In winter it frequents birches and alders, copses, and areas along streams, visiting suburban gardens in severe weather.

Migration
When winter closes in, the siskin is forced to migrate south. Birds bred in Scotland move down into England and, in severe winters, many birds from Scandinavia migrate into southern Europe and to the Midlands and South of England. These birds, unused to man, are very tame and can be approached to within a few feet. In England they can often be seen feeding at bird tables, especially on peanuts, from January to March.

Flight

Like other finches, siskins have a slow, undulating flight, gliding with wings closed between each few wing beats. They are capable of fast flight over short distances when threatened.

Lifespan

Although not predated to the same extent as some of the other finches, losses are heavy in winter and during migration. Very few ever manage to breed for more than a single season.

Main Foods

When returning from winter quarters, siskins settle in areas where spruce trees are plentiful. In May the crop is ripe, and the youngsters in the first nest are reared mainly on spruce seeds, with insects and weed seeds. Spruce seeds are followed by pine cones, which open later. Siskins also forage in fields and hedgerows. When the pine cones are finished the birds move into the birch forests until autumn. In winter they feed on

Meadowsweet

alders, primarily the cones, and later from the ground. Throughout the year their main foods are small insects, spruce, pine, dandelion, elm, dock, birch, hardheads, thistles, meadowsweet, mugwort, alder and larch.

Siskin distribution in Great Britain

Flocking

In the breeding season pairs roost together near the nest site but, in winter, siskins roost in flocks, generally in tall conifers or thorn scrub. They feed in flocks, usually of 30 to 50, all the year round. When feeding in trees they behave very similarly to tits, continually on the move from tree to tree.

Courtship and Territory

In courtship the siskin adopts similar wing-dropping, body-swaying and tail-spreading movements to the goldfinch. The cock also raises his black crown and yellow rump feathers and fluffs his breast. Between these displays the cock sings from the tree tops. Cocks start to make up to the hens in the winter flock about February. By the end of March they are usually paired and the cock is feeding the hen. Like all Cardueline finches, siskins nest in small, loose colonies of three or four pairs and only defend a small area around the nest, feeding outside the territory with the flock.

Adult siskin hen

Dark-eyed brown siskin hen

Nesting
Siskins build a tiny, compact nest high up in conifers, usually out on a branch in a relatively exposed position. The nest is made of moss, lichens and grasses, and lined with hair and feathers. Two broods are normal.

Eggs
The siskin usually lays four or five eggs. These are bluish white with pale reddish spots and streaks, similar to, but smaller than, those of the goldfinch.

Laying and Incubation

One egg is laid each day, usually in the morning before 9.00. Incubation is by the hen alone and commences when the fourth egg has been laid. During this period the cock feeds the hen, who only leaves the nest for a few minutes about three times a day to defecate, drink and perhaps bathe.

Young

The young hatch after about 12 days from when the hen starts to sit, but in cold damp weather may take one or two days longer. The young are naked, blind and helpless. The cock continues to feed the hen, and the hen feeds the young for the first seven days. During this period the hen cleans the nest, either eating the faeces or carrying them away. At seven days old the nestlings' eyes are open and their feathers are starting to grow. They are now large enough to generate some heat themselves, so the hen is able to leave them sometimes and help the cock forage for food. She will continue to brood them between times, especially at night. At this age the young are large enough to excrete onto the rim of the nest, so the hen ceases to clean it.

Fledging

At 13 days old the young may be fully feathered, although the tail is not fully grown. In bad weather, the parents cannot collect as much food, so it may be another three or four days before the young reach this stage. The young leave the nest between 13 and 17 days from hatching, and hop about in nearby trees. The parents continue to feed them for several more days, after which the hen starts to build the second nest. The cock feeds the young for a few more days, and then they join the main flock and are self-supporting.

Single factor, brown-pastel siskin hen

Moult

Young siskins moult into their adult colours at about 12 weeks old. Late hatched young often moult at a slightly younger age, so that they all moult at about the same time. Adults normally moult in September in the same way as other finches.

The moult is necessary because, after a year, a bird's feathers become worn and are less effective for flight and insulation. In most birds the moult occurs outside the breeding and migration seasons, but while food is still sufficiently plentiful to support the growth of feathers. However, we do not know exactly what brings on the moult. Reducing daylight length has some effect and perhaps colder nights. Nevertheless, not all birds of any given species finish breeding at the same time, although it is not unknown for a pair to commence a late nest only to abandon it while young are still in the nest and start moulting immediately.

Adult finches replace all their feathers after breeding. Sexual activities cease within a matter of days. The birds become silent and keep mostly in cover. Gonads regress and the sex hormones are replaced

Adult siskin cock

by other hormones. The thyroid hormone raises the birds' metabolic rate and controls the growth of new feathers, which are fed from the blood stream, while the skin becomes heavily vascularised instead of being loose and thin.

Feathers are grouped into tracts that run along the length of the body with bare areas of skin in between, as can easily be seen in nestlings. In nestlings, all the feathers grow at the same time until they spread over the whole body. In adults, new feathers emerge in a regular sequence over a period of several weeks. When one feather is grown, the next is shed, so that the bird is never left naked or unable to fly. (Ducks, geese and swans

Sowthistle

have a different arrangement.) If feathers are knocked out accidentally outside the moulting season, replacement feathers grow immediately, but not if a feather is just broken. Each growing feather is encased in a sheath or quill containing blood. When the feather is about one third grown it breaks the sheath, which shrinks and finally drops away. Within a few days of the feather completing its growth it hardens, the blood supply stops, and it becomes a dead structure held by the muscles at its base.

In adult finches the first feathers to be shed are the innermost primaries and the outermost secondaries of both wings, the last in each wing being the outermost primaries and the innermost secondaries. The large tail feathers are moulted in pairs, beginning with the central pair. Body feathers are moulted from the centre of each feather tract spreading outwards. In their first moult, juveniles retain their large flight and tail feathers for another year. Apart from this they moult their feathers in the same sequence as adults. Most juveniles moult when they are about 12 weeks old, but late hatched birds moult before that age, when the adults are moulting.

Feathers consist almost exclusively of keratins, which are proteins containing large amounts of sulphur amino-acids, cystine and methionine. For this reason the birds require a great deal of protein during the moult, which has to come from the food that the birds eat at the time. The true nutritional requirements to provide this are not yet known. The food must be available continuously. Any shortage on even one day is sufficient to cause the formation of a fault bar on the growing feather, which is then liable to break at this point during the year. As well as producing new feathers, the bird loses heat much more easily while moulting and therefore must eat more. Adults generally take up to 12 weeks to moult completely, usually beginning in August or September.

Dandelion

Feather Type
In most species, including finches, there are two feather types, and a bird has either one or the other.
- A jonque has shorter, narrow, silky feathers that are much better coloured and make the bird look brighter but smaller. This is generally known by aviculturists as a 'yellow', but this name is very misleading, because it does not refer to the colour of the bird.
- A mealy has longer, broader, coarser feathers, the tips of which are pale buff or white. The bird has a mealy appearance, but looks larger and has a duller appearance than the jonque. This is generally known by aviculturists as a 'buff', but again it is misleading, because it has no direct connection with the colour of the bird, but with its feather type.

In some species it is not easy to tell the difference, but this does not apply to the siskin, in which both types occur and are generally fairly easy to distinguish.

Lifestyle in the Wild -
Goldfinches

Order: Passeriformes
Family: Fringillidae (Finches)
Genus: *Carduelis*
Species: *Carduelis carduelis brittanica*
Common Name: Goldfinch

Description
    Length: 11.5cm (4.5in)
    Weight: 28.35g (1oz)
    Wing Span: 17.75cm (7in)
    Tarsus: 1.5cm (0.6in)

Cock
Predominantly buff and chestnut on the back and flanks and whitish on the belly, with a red face mask (blaze), greyish-white cheeks, black crown, and side stripes extending from the nape, almost forming a collar. Its wings are black, with a broad, brilliant yellow bar and white tips like buttons on each of the primary feathers. The forked tail is also black, with white tips on the upper side of each feather and broad white patches like half-moons on the underside of the two outer pairs. The red blaze usually extends to the back of the eye. See photograph on page 29.

Hen
Similar to the cock, but slightly smaller. The red blaze usually extends only to the centre of the eye. The black crown nearly always has some brown flecking. The wing butts and bristles at the base of the beak are brown or grey, whereas these areas are black in an adult cock. First year cocks often have some brown on the crown and wing butts. Not an easy bird to sex without experience.

Juveniles
Streaked, and lacking the red, white and black on the head, but having wing and tail markings similar to the adult. They generally have more grey on them, and are known as grey-pates.

Bill

The bill is long, thin and pointed, enabling the bird to feed on prickly plants like thistles and teasels. No doubt the bristles at the base of the bill are to protect its nostrils and face as it probes for the seeds. It has the same grooves in the upper mandible and chisel edge on the lower mandible as other finches. The hen has a smaller

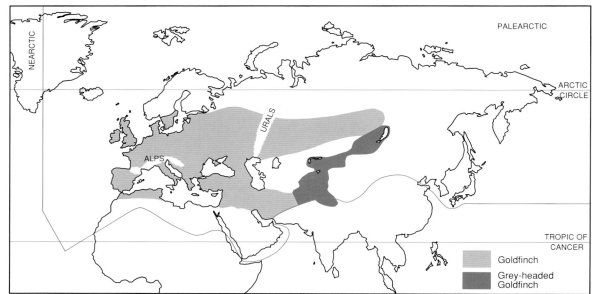

Goldfinch distribution world-wide

bill (generally considered to be 1mm shorter than that of the cock). The bill has a black tip extending up the beak but, as the birds come into breeding condition, the black disappears, leaving the bill a clear bone colour.

Legs and Feet

In the resident birds these are black, but in the migrating birds they can be much lighter, sometimes almost white. The goldfinch has short legs and comparatively large, strong feet, enabling it to hang upside-down, like a tit, on food plants. It only rarely descends to ground level to feed, although hens sometimes take teasel seeds dropped onto the ground by the cock, who is able to extract the seeds more easily with his longer beak.

Crop

Goldfinches have the same extendible gullet as the other Cardueline finches, enabling them to store food that is afterwards regurgitated to feed a partner or youngsters.

Distribution

Goldfinches breed in most of the western part of Eurasia, from North Africa to Southern Scandinavia. They are well distributed throughout the British Isles, except for the northern part of Scotland, but more plentiful in the southern half of England and Wales.

Habitat
In autumn and winter goldfinches are found on open ground where there are weeds (especially thistles), rough ground, neglected pastures, roadsides and wasteland. In the breeding season they nest in gardens, orchards and open cultivated land with a sprinkling of trees and tall bushes, returning to the open ground to feed.

Migration
Goldfinches resident in the British Isles never move very far from where they are hatched except in very severe weather, when they are forced southwards to find food. In addition to our residents, it is worth looking out for the following:

- A variation generally whiter than our own, particularly around the face and nape, with a darker red blaze. These birds can also have larger wing spots and light-coloured legs. They generally winter in Iberia, but often arrive on our east coast in winter and then move inland.
- In April, others arrive on the south coast and spread inland, departing in September. Many of these spring arrivals have almost black wings, lacking the distinct buttons of our residents and winter visitors.

Flight
The goldfinch has the graceful, undulating flight of the finches and, when feeding, flutters butterfly-like about the seed heads.

Lifespan
Like all birds, goldfinches sustain heavy losses among young birds from predators, and among both old and young in the winter when the food supply runs out. Only about 25% of young birds survive long enough to breed, and those that do are not likely to live longer than 18 months.

Goldfinch distribution in the British Isles

Main Foods
Chickweed, groundsel, dandelion, coltsfoot, elm, ragwort, goatsbeard, hawksbeard, sowthistle, thistles, hardheads, wall lettuce, teasel, meadowsweet, burdock, birch, alder and pine.

Flocking
At the end of the breeding season family parties join together and roam the countryside in search of food. Flocks of 20 to 30 are common and the goldfinches are sometimes joined by siskins and redpolls. At night

Peathroat goldfinch

they roost in evergreens, and by day they take a circular route, feeding at the same times and places while food stocks last. As the daylight increases and weather improves, they start to form into pairs while remaining in the flock.

Courtship and Territory

Courtship display consists mainly of swinging from side to side, dropping the wings and spreading the tail to show off the colours. This is accompanied by the 'swee-et' call. Both sexes indulge in this behaviour. Since they are late nesters, territory is not taken up until the end of April and early May. The pair only defends a small territory around the nest and continues to feed with the flock. The cock selects a prominent twig close to the chosen nesting site and sings from this whenever the pair visit the site. Several pairs will often nest in a loose colony, particularly if they do not feed near the nest.

Nesting

Goldfinches build neat, small and compact nests, made chiefly of mosses and lichens and lined with the down of thistles and other plants. The nest is usually in a rosette of small twigs at the top of a bush or small tree, or on the outer branches of larger trees. It is deep, to retain the eggs in windy weather, and bound together with spiders' web silk. The building may take anything from two to fourteen days, depending on how near the hen is to laying. Two broods are normal.

Laying and Incubation

Laying commences in early May. Four or five (occasionally six) bluish-white eggs, spotted and streaked with reddish brown, form a clutch. The eggs are very similar to those of the siskin, redpoll and linnet, except in size. One is laid each day, usually in the morning. Incubation commences in earnest when the fourth egg has been laid, and is by the hen

Goldfinch cock

alone. The cock goes off to the feeding grounds, which may be as much as two miles away, fills his crop, and returns to feed the hen, sits on his twig, renders his song and then goes off to feed again. Twice or three times a day, the hen will leave the nest for a few minutes to defecate, preen and sometimes bathe, but she is usually accompanied by the cock. The eggs hatch in 13 to 15 days, depending on the weather and temperature. The young take several hours to hatch and, when they are dry, the shells are carried away by the hen.

Young

When they first hatch, the cock feeds the hen, and the hen feeds the youngsters by regurgitating food from the crop. At this period, quite a large proportion of the food is small insects such as greenfly and gnats, as well as half-ripe seeds with water and some grit. The hen fills the crops of the young, which lasts them until their next feed, about half an hour later. Goldfinches always rear more young in warm, dry summers than in cold,

Northern goldfinch

wet summers, presumably because of the availability of the small insects. The hen broods the young and cleans the nest for the first seven days or so, by which time they are large enough to generate heat themselves and can defecate onto the rim of the nest. The young stay in the nest for approximately 14 days, depending on the weather, by which time they are fully feathered, although the tail is not fully grown.

Fledging

When they leave the nest the young can fly, but they take a few days to become proficient. The parents continue to feed them for at least 10 days, sometimes longer. Young goldfinches seem to have difficulty in becoming self-supporting. They do not obtain their full colours until the first moult.

Moult

Young goldfinches moult at approximately 12 weeks, though late hatchers may moult out sooner. Adults start to moult at the end of September and replace their feathers in the same way as siskins (see Chapter 3).

Feather Type

There are both jonque (intensive colour) and mealy (non-intensive) feather types in goldfinches, but these can be difficult to distinguish and are of less importance than in some other species.

Accommodation and Foods

ACCOMMODATION

We have already discussed the minimum suitable size of cage in chapter 1 but, as well as providing room for living and breeding, we must consider the need to ring the young if they are to be sold or exhibited. It is best to make the cage so that it can be divided when required. The birds should always have food and water at one end and the nesting site at the other. The parents can then be shut in the feeding end while the young are ringed, and will not be disturbed to the same extent. At the same time, the breeder will have more freedom for the ringing operation.

Siskins can be bred in a cage 2m x 0.5m x 0.5m (6ft x 18in x 18in) or slightly smaller though, if a larger cage can be provided, so much the better. They are accommodating little birds who, in the wild, generally nest out in the open. In cages and aviaries they usually nest up against the wires if they can. Since they are very tame, this does not generally cause any problems, but safeguard against cats, owls and hawks. A wicker basket fastened onto the cage wires with a few sprigs of evergreen around it will normally be quite satisfactory. Again, it is useful to be able to shut the parents into the other half of the cage when ringing the chicks.

Goldfinches, on the other hand, are very shy and timid when breeding and as large a cage as possible is advised, if possible, 3m x 1m x 1m high (9ft x 3ft x 3ft). One end should be screened to give the hen privacy while nesting and it is certainly better if the parents can be shut off while the young are ringed. Goldfinches will not usually accept interference. Inspections should be kept to the minimum necessary for the keeping of satisfactory records. When a pair choose a site and begin building a nest, resist any temptation to inspect it. Interference at this stage will almost certainly result in the hen seeking a new nesting site. Once the hen begins serious incubation she usually tolerates very discreet inspections, preferably when she vacates the nest of her own accord to feed or defecate.

The inquisitiveness of some cocks can be a problem at this time in a confined space, and may lead to eggs being broken and eaten. This habit, once started, is very difficult to break. With such cocks the provision of a divider is essential, but you should only use a wire one, so that the pair can still see and have contact with each other. Denial of this contact

Cheveral goldfinch

can lead to a loss of condition in some cocks, and they sometimes even die.

Too much interference causes the birds either to desert the nest or to throw out the young on, or shortly after, hatching. The screening used for the nesting sites should let in light, but be thick enough to prevent the hen from being seen easily. A good bunch of suitable evergreen should be fixed behind the screen, leaving a space of 15cm to 25cm between the top of the bunch and the top of the cage; they usually build the nest in the top of the bunch. Watch out for egg shells on the floor of the cage so that you know when the young have hatched and can work out when to ring them.

Siskins and goldfinches can be mixed with other species of finches in aviaries as long as they are not over-crowded. However, during the breeding season it is best to avoid mixing with bullfinches, buntings, bramblings or chaffinches, as these can be very pugnacious at this time.

Goldfinches can be bred on the colony system (two or three pairs together) provided that the sexes are equal in number and the aviary is large enough. However, better breeding results are often obtained by having only one pair each of a few species. It is advisable to have only one pair of siskins in any aviary because cock siskins fight each other when in breeding condition, although they very rarely interfere with other species. The best results with both species are obtained when one pair of birds is given an aviary to itself, but the minimum satisfactory size is 2m x 1m x 2m (6ft x 3ft x 6ft), because it is necessary enter the aviary periodically for management reasons. Since this is rather expensive in materials and space, most fanciers prefer to have a larger aviary housing several different species. Allow approximately 2.2 cubic metres (80 cubic feet) of space per pair. When several pairs are housed in one aviary, plenty of individual nesting sites or an artificial hedge are satisfactory and the birds nest quite close to each other without fighting.

FOOD
Seeds

When several different species are housed together, seed mixtures can be quite useful; what one species does not like, others will probably eat. However, you must ensure that the mixture contains sufficient quantities of the seed needed by each of the species you are keeping. If it does not, you can supplement by supplying such seeds in separate pots.

Curled dock

Although wild siskins feed more on tree seeds than goldfinches do, under domestic conditions they eat many of the seeds in a good British Finch mixture, so can be fed the same base main diet. Extra nutritional seeds can be added. Many of these will be found in a good British condition mixture, and others can be added to the mix or supplied in separate containers.

Niger: This is very important to goldfinches and siskins. Mixtures do not usually contain enough, so extra should be added or supplied separately. Warning: use limited quantities, since it can be fattening if consumed in large amounts.

Hemp: This is particularly important to goldfinches, who can be allowed to consume fair quantities without fear of obesity. Hemp is also important to siskins, but only in limited amounts, because they are prone to obesity.

Maw Seed: Because it is very small, maw seed usually gets lost in mixtures. It is best supplied separately in a small pot or mixed with soft foods. Siskins are especially fond of this seed, which appears to have medicinal properties.

Teasel: An important winter food, easily digested, and also very useful during the rearing season. Being very expensive it is rarely included in any mixtures. It is best fed separately or mixed with soft foods.

Pine Nuts: These are part of the siskin's natural diet and should be fed separately. Both species can be given small quantities of the small Chinese type.

Soaked Seeds: Seeds that have been soaked in cold water for 24 to 48 hours should be supplied regularly, especially in the breeding season. These can be mixed with soft foods. You should wash the seeds several times during soaking, giving a final rinse and allowing them to drain before feeding.

Egg Food, Soft Food or Rearing Food

Both siskins and goldfinches usually take these freely. Any that do not soon learn to take any of the brands of egg food normally fed to canaries if you keep a few canaries with them during the winter period or when young birds are first weaned. If they give these foods to their young it will be a great help in the rearing of fine, healthy stock.

Mealworms

Mealworms provide a suitable animal protein and siskins especially take them very readily.

Mealworms are best offered as a titbit in the spring, one or two per bird, with soft food. They should be broken or beheaded to immobilise them. The birds do not usually consume the whole mealworm, but extract the contents, leaving the skin.

Do not provide an unlimited supply: too many mealworms can have a detrimental effect on both young and adults, being very high in proteins but lacking in calcium.

Double-factor brown-pastel siskin pair

Grit

Seed eaters need grit to grind food in their gizzards to digest it, especially when you give them dry seeds. They should always have a plentiful supply. A good mineralised grit also contains certain beneficial trace elements.

Water

Clean water must be supplied daily for both drinking and bathing. Birds need to bathe regularly to keep their plumage in good condition. Bathing also helps to bring them into breeding condition.

Wild Foods

Coltsfoot, dandelion, chickweed, groundsel, ragwort, mugwort, thistles, hardheads, teasel, wall lettuce, meadowsweet, burdock and many other wild foods should be supplied in quantity whenever available, but take care that they have not been contaminated in any way. The birds also obtain many small insects from these foods, and these too are beneficial.

Supplements

As has already been explained, a bird's exact requirements are not known, but few additives are needed if a full and varied diet is provided throughout the year. However, some breeders add various supplements to the main foods in an effort to overcome possible shortages, particularly in vitamins and minerals. Care should be taken not to exceed the recommended quantities.

ABIDEC*: This is a very useful vitamin supplement and is best added to the drinking water. There are many other useful multi-vitamin type supplements on the market, any one of which should meet your birds' needs.

Cod Liver Oil: This is a rich source of vitamin D and can be given throughout the breeding season and during the moult. One teaspoonful is mixed thoroughly with one pound of seed, which is allowed to stand for 24 hours before being fed to the birds.

PYM*: Yeast can be mixed with seed in almost any quantities, as can mineral mixtures, especially those containing iodine. These are a good help in maintaining healthy condition.

Tonics: These can be useful, especially the ones containing iron.

Probiotics: These encourage and build up the 'friendly' bacteria whose function is to keep all the 'unfriendly' bacteria in the gut in check. Probiotics can be given daily throughout the year in the drinking water. (Dosage: in accordance with the manufacturer's instructions.)

* Registered Trade Mark

Silverbirch

Single-factor pastel siskin cock

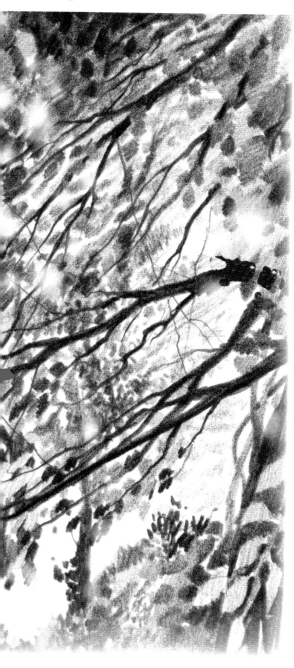

Breeding

Pairing

In the wild both siskins and goldfinches pair up while they are in the winter flocks. Under domestic conditions best results are obtained by putting the selected pairs together during the winter instead of waiting until they are in breeding condition. They then come into breeding condition together and settle down more easily when put into their breeding quarters in the early summer. Both species are late breeders in the wild, commencing in May, but with good feeding in aviaries will often start nesting in April. If the weather is mild in early spring, siskins often start very early.

Nesting

Siskins nest in the open and will not use thick cover. For this reason, they frequently build their nest against the outside netting of their aviary. This makes it difficult to give them enough protection. A nesting site that usually attracts them can be made by erecting a pole in a clear space in the aviary with a 60cm square (2ft square) cover of wood or similar material fastened immediately above it on the top of the aviary. Two good sized branches of conifer are fixed horizontally onto the pole, one at the top and one below it, leaving about 23cm (9in) clear between the two. Siskins generally build on the bottom branch. In cages, a wicker nest basket fixed to the front of the cage with a few sprigs of suitable evergreen usually attracts them.

Goldfinches take to similar sites, but like to nest at the top of a bush, usually in a rosette of small twigs. The nest is generally well hidden. Again, a good branch of conifer is very useful, but this time it should be fixed vertically, leaving about 23cm (9in) between it and the top of the aviary. If the aviary has an open wire top, some cover should be placed on top of the aviary to protect the birds from the worst elements of weather and other dangers.

Both species build neat little nests and should be supplied with small twigs, moss, rootlets, vegetable down, cow and dog hair, and sizal string teased out and cut into 5cm (2in) lengths. Cotton wool always attracts them and must be supplied in a roll tightly tied with string or wire so that they can only pull out beakfuls at a time. If they can get larger quantities there is a grave risk that they will get their feet tangled in it with dire consequences. White cotton kapoc is a better choice. All base materials must be supplied damp;

otherwise the birds cannot mould them to shape. A little dry material to line the nest should also be supplied.

The finished nest is usually strong and substantial, but some hens, especially siskins, build a flimsy one or start laying before it is finished. In such cases, the eggs fall to the floor. A small wicker cane basket in which she can construct her nest helps to prevent these losses.

Brooding

When the third or fourth egg has been laid the hen begins to sit. Brooding is by the hen alone, who will come off the nest a few times during the daytime to defecate, have a drink and perhaps a bathe, generally accompanied by the cock. The cock spends his time displaying and feeding, filling his crop and returning to feed the hen by regurgitation. The eggs hatch in approximately 13 days but may take a little longer in cold weather. Egg shells on the aviary floor will show when the young have hatched; this will cause less upset to the parents than continually examining the nest.

Siskins quite frequently commence incubation early, often from when the first or second egg is laid. If they are left to their own devices this can result in chicks with considerable age differences in the same brood. This in turn can result in the largest chick being the only one to be reared. Fortunately, siskins generally do not mind a little interference: with experience, the problem

Single-factor brown-pastel siskin cock

can be overcome by substituting a dummy for each egg until the third or fourth egg has been laid, ensuring a more equal hatch.

Rearing

As already stated, goldfinches desert the nest or throw out the young when they are small if you show too much interest. Do not attempt to ring the young until they are about six days old. Siskins are much more obliging, and can usually be ringed at five days without problems.

In the first few days the cocks feed the hens and the hens feed the young. They will be looking for small insects such as gnats, particularly aphids. A patch of nettles in the flight is a great help in this respect, and so is a pile of horse or cow manure and rotting fruit, especially bananas. Roses or other suitable vegetation can be grown up the outside of the wire. All this encourages aphids, small flies, and other insects, providing animal protein. It is no use planting them inside the flight; most finches will eat the young shoots, killing the plants.

Both species accept mealworms when rearing chicks, but numbers fed must be restricted, because mealworms are lacking in calcium. About 30 a day at the peak of rearing is the maximum, decreasing soon after the chicks fledge.

Siskin hen feeding 11-day-old chicks

They will also be looking for semi-ripe seeds and green vegetation. For this reason, all favourite wild seeds and plants that can be collected should be supplied, especially chickweed, sow or milkthistle and groundsel. Groundsel keeps better placed in jars of water; otherwise it quickly dies and becomes useless. Soaked seed and egg food also play an important part in the rearing of the young. When collecting wild foods, take great care that they have not been sprayed with insecticides or herbicides, both of which can be lethal to birds.

As the young grow and start to feather, they can generate heat in the nest themselves, enabling the hen to have more time with the cock to collect food. The hen cleans all the faeces from the nest for the first seven days, by which time the young are large enough to excrete onto the rim of the nest. At about this time the hen ceases to brood the young during the day, but will continue to brood at night for a few more days.

At 14 days old the young are fully feathered and ready to fledge, although their flight and tail feathers are not quite fully grown. The hen may start to build another nest, but the cock usually goes on feeding the young until the second brood starts to hatch. Both species, especially goldfinches, take a long time to wean and are best left with their parents until they have moulted. Taking the young away too soon can result in losses.

Some siskin cocks, although attentive to the hen, fail to feed their young. If this happens the hen must be allowed to continue feeding. She will be reluctant to do this if she is brooding a second clutch. It may, therefore, be necessary to remove the cock, the second clutch of eggs or both to ensure that the first nestlings are fully weaned.

Honeysuckle

Moult

The young moult out into adult plumage at about 12 weeks old, but do not moult their flight and tail feathers until their second moult. This is when they need all the wild seeds you can get. All kinds of thistles, teasels and hardheads help goldfinches in particular to bring out their full colours.

Colour Feeding

This is not recommended for either species. Good natural colour can be achieved on the varied diet previously described. Purity of colour is essential if they are to do well on the show bench. In the case of the goldfinch some breeders use partial colour feeding to enhance the blaze. Such feeding has to be done carefully since the yellow flash in the wings can very easily be turned orange, spoiling the effect. Colour food must be withheld until the bird has almost finished moulting, when only the head feathers which are last to moult are left. Infuse a quarter of a teaspoonful of ™Caraphil Red (Roche Products Ltd) with a little boiling water in a suitable container, diluting this by adding approximately one litre of cold water and mixing thoroughly. This diluted mixture is given to the bird in place of normal drinking water. The water should be changed each day until the moult has been completed.

Teasel

Chapter 7

Ringing Birds

The siskin and the goldfinch are both on Schedule 3 Part 1 of the Wild Life and Countryside Act 1981. For this reason, although it is permissible to keep them if they are not ringed, it is illegal to buy, sell or exhibit unringed specimens. There are two approved legal rings:

- The British Bird Council ring, which is exclusive to the British Bird fancy.
- The IOA ring, which is used for different types of birds and by exhibitors who may wish to send their birds to shows abroad. At present, quarantine and import/export regulations make exhibiting abroad very difficult. However, closer ties with Europe could see some beneficial changes in the regulations.

The British Bird Council ring is brown, and the letters 'BC' are stamped across it, followed by a size letter and serial number. Since 1991 rings also carry a year date. A great deal of work has been done over the years to find the best size for each species, and for the two species under discussion these are as follows:

- Siskin: code size B
- Goldfinch: code size C

This ring has to be put on the young bird while it is still in the nest and is acceptable to the authorities as proof that the bird is aviary-bred.

One problem with the closed ring is that some birds resent either the interference in the nest or the foreign object on the chicks. For this reason, the parent birds must be accustomed to the owner and, if possible, reasonably tame before the breeding season. Ringing of the chicks should take place between five and seven days, depending on the rate of growth of the young and the breeder's experience. The siskin is far more tolerant of inspections of the nest at this critical time, and little trouble will be experienced in ringing the majority of the young; five days of age will usually prove satisfactory. The goldfinch does not take so kindly to nest inspections, so it is best to leave the ringing of this species as late as possible; six or even seven days is more satisfactory. An inexperienced breeder will probably have to ring earlier than one who is more used to it. The later ringing takes place, the less are the chances of rejection. This is because the hen no longer needs to remove the faecal sacs from the nest once the chicks start to void their faeces over the side of the nest, so she is no longer so meticulous in cleaning out the nest.

Rings that are fitted too early come off in the nest and are lost. If the ring can be removed easily after fitting it is best to leave it for a further day or two. This can arise particularly when the growth of chicks is staggered because they have hatched on different days. There are usually fewer problems with owner-bred hens than with bought-in stock. With newly-purchased hens it is best to be cautious and ring only the largest chick in the nest to begin with. If this is not mutilated or rejected, it is usually safe to ring the rest of the chicks. However, if all is not well, do not attempt to ring the remaining chicks under this hen. These chicks will either have to be left un-ringed or fostered out to a more reliable hen. Many breeders have a few pairs of canaries to act as foster parents in such cases.

The actual time of day chosen to ring chicks will depend on the breeder's own circumstances. Some breeders like to ring towards dusk in the belief that the hen will settle down on the ringed chicks. However, if she is going to reject them, she will undoubtedly do so when cleaning the nest the following morning. For this reason, some breeders like to ring in the early morning so that a watch can be kept on the hen. If she rejects, the chicks can be picked up before they expire and either put back with their rings removed or fostered out. If a hen accepts her chicks being ringed, it really makes little difference what time of day you ring them. However, it is sensible to provide some rearing food or favourite seeding weeds to keep the hen busy while you ring the chicks.

For the inexperienced breeder, who will undoubtedly take some time to complete the ringing operation, it is best to leave one chick in the nest. The remainder can be removed and placed in a lined canary nest pan or something similar. Leaving one chick in the nest prevents the hen from being concerned if she returns before ringing is completed. Do not expect to ring chicks easily the first time that you try. It takes practice and experience to become proficient at the task. Many breeders find it necessary to ring the birds before they are seven days old, but they should be aware of the problems. It is well worth practising on canaries and budgerigars, which are much more tolerant of interference.

The recommended method for ringing is as follows (see illustrations below):
- As you look at the rings you will see that they are tapered slightly (caused by stamping the number on them). Always place the big end on first.
- It is essential to get the three long toes straight and parallel to each other. If the toes are crossed the ring will not go on. Sometimes it takes several goes to get the ring in this position (fig 1) because the young bird continually tries to clench its toes.
- A gentle pressure and slight twisting motion will now take the ring up over the ball of the foot (figs 2 and 3).
- The ring is then slid up the shank of the leg until the hind claw is released (figs 4 and 5).

Do not try to rush the job; it requires care and patience.

| Fig 1 | Fig 2 | Fig 3 | Fig 4 | Fig 5 |

Ringing young birds

Exhibition

The most important rule if you are to be successful on the show bench is to ensure that your birds have access to water for regular bathing. Some birds are reluctant to bathe, but usually follow suit when they see or hear other birds doing so. If they will not, or do not have access to bathing facilities, they should be sprayed regularly. Many successful exhibitors spray their birds if necessary, but prefer a bird to bathe naturally. The majority will, if given the opportunity. When a bird bathes, it relaxes, allowing the water to penetrate the feather; when sprayed, it behaves as if it is trying to avoid the water, 'tightening up'. Birds soon accept spraying, however, and many look forward to and enjoy it. Without any doubt, rain water is best for their plumage. This is what wild birds use and they always carry a 'sheen' or gloss on the feather, obtained by bathing frequently.

A bird should get used to its show cage before it is exhibited. Some birds take to a show cage 'like a duck to water' as the saying goes, but others do not like to be confined. Such birds should be run into show cages for very short periods initially; eventually they will get accustomed to them. Occasionally one does meet a problem bird, but it is surprising how it will accept a show cage in time. Very often a bird, when shown at a small show for a few hours, gains confidence. Once acquired, it is never lost.

Some birds - just a few - have a nasty habit of facing the back of the cage. Such birds seldom overcome the habit. The ideal exhibition bird always faces the front of the cage. Any bird that proves difficult will need patience. Never push a bird so hard that you destroy its confidence. A few will never be steady enough for showing and these are best kept purely for breeding purposes. In addition to this, both the goldfinch and the siskin tend to use the wire front of the show cage too much so must be trained if they are to 'work' the perches correctly. Goldfinches in particular can also develop the nervous habit of 'twirling', a wry movement of the neck that can be very difficult to cure, even with great patience and experience. Again, such nervous birds are probably best left in the breeding pen.

When dealing with current-year birds, you should limit their training to short periods at first, returning them immediately after each session to their normal living quarters. Young birds are much more vulnerable to stress than adults, and losses will be experienced if they are put under too much stress too early in their lives. Never be in too much of a hurry to steady down that promising youngster. Patience is the key if you want to avoid disappointments.

The staging or presentation of British seedeaters, mules and hybrids is very important if the exhibitor is to be successful. There is a slight difference in the sizes of show cages advocated by the Scottish British Bird and

Satinette canary x goldfinch mule hen

Near-clear, light goldfinch mule

Mule Club, but we are all agreed that green is the acceptable colour for interiors and black for exteriors. It is very important that exhibits are staged in the sizes advocated for the particular species. It is always permissible to use a larger cage but never a smaller one. Please remember that the sizes recommended and adopted are the minimum sizes and, in the main, the most suitable.

It is most important that show cages are made by skilled cage makers who specialise in this particular job. It is also very important that internal and external decoration of the show cage is of the highest standard. Sometimes we see show cages that are poorly constructed and decorated. A good bird deserves a good cage; it certainly enhances a bird's chances on the show bench.

To maintain show cages in good condition it is important that you always clean them after a show; wash them thoroughly, particularly the perches, and place them in your carrying case ready for your next show. They also need repainting periodically. If a little polish is put on the cage prior to the show, cleaning with warm water is easy afterwards.

It must be pointed out to those just beginning to exhibit that the birds are only allowed to be kept in show cages for 72 hours and while being transported to and from the shows. Also, it is only permissible to confine a bird in a show cage for training for a maximum of one hour in any 24. At other times, the birds must be kept in their aviaries or in the recommended stock cages.

Knapweed

Show Cage

The correct show cage for both the siskin and the goldfinch is No 2:

	Length	Height	Depth
English Pattern	28cm (11in)	24cm (9.5in)	11.5cm (4^{1}/$_{2}$in)
Scottish Pattern	25cm (10in)	24cm (9.5in)	11.5cm (4^{1}/$_{2}$in)

Gauge wires: No 14, set at 1.5cm (^{5}/$_{8}$in) centres.

Drinking hole: 2cm (^{3}/$_{4}$in) diameter

Bottom rail: 3.75 cm (1^{1}/$_{2}$in) high

Top rail: (shaped) 2.5cm (1in) at the outside, sloping to 1.25cm (^{1}/$_{2}$in) at the centre.

Painted: Brolac Georgian Green inside, on the outside of the wires and on both top and bottom rails, and the drinker. Glossy black outside top, bottom, back and sides.

Breed Standard - Siskin

An exhibition siskin should have good type, purity of colour, well-defined markings and be of good size. The standard is as follows:

Size: Large as possible. 10 Points

Type: Nicely rounded full head, cobby well-filled body. 10 Points

Colour and Markings: Rich even colour throughout, green above, yellow below, well-defined, faintly laced black cap, and reasonably well-defined bib.

Plantain Ribwort

Heather

Tansy

Distinct working on back and down the flanks. Well-defined yellow in wings and tail. Hens: greyish and yellow, lacking black cap and bib. Must have profuse working on head, back and flanks, and carried well into chest. 55 Points
Feather Quality and Condition: 10 Points
Steadiness and Presentation: 15 Points
Total: 100 Points

> **Notes:** Yellows and buffs are very evident in this species. Buffs though of less intensive colour must excel in type and workings.
> **Faults:** Smokiness, poor or impure colour over working in cocks. Lack of working in hens, eye defects, deformities, poor presentation, and insufficiently trained.

Breed Standard - Goldfinch

An exhibition goldfinch must be of good size, well-proportioned and bold. A large, expansive, square, clean-cut blaze is most desirable. Well-defined markings on wings and tail known as buttons and moons are important. The standard is as follows:

Size: Large as possible. 10 Points
Type: Nicely rounded full head, well-filled, cone-shaped body of bold and upstanding appearance with plenty of swagger and swank. 10 Points
Colour and Markings: Expansive, clean-cut, square blaze of bright, rich, vermilion red, extending well behind the eye into forehead and well down the throat. Broad, solid, well-defined head markings. Rich brown tannings on breast and flanks, extending well down. All contrasting well on whitish body. Rich brown back with even, well-defined, whitish buttons and bright yellow wing flash. Tail black with well-defined whitish buttons and moons. Hens similar, but less extensive blaze colour, not so bright or clean-cut. Head often grizzled or flecked with brown. 55 Points
Feather Quality and Condition: 15 Points
Steadiness and Presentation: 10 Points
Total: 100 Points

> **Notes:** Tendency for hens to be smaller than cocks. Hens and also current year cocks may show brown flecking or grizzling on the head, which is permissible.
>
> **Faults:** Too much black in the blaze, particularly around the base of the mandible and eyes, showing black gutteral lines or other impurities, flecking or grizzling on head or white spreading into nape. Eye defects, deformities, poor presentation, insufficiently trained.

Cinnamon goldfinch hen

Lightly-marked, light goldfinch mule

Mules and Hybrids

Mule is the fancier's term for offspring raised from a canary and a British finch; offspring from two British finches of different species are referred to as *hybrids*. Both types are really hybrids, and some show schedules refer to mules as canary hybrids. Mules and hybrids are bred for exhibition, song or ornamental purposes and are generally considered to be infertile. However, modern knowledge and the production of the red canary from the red-hooded siskin of South America suggest that some mules may be fertile when paired back to canaries, but perhaps not until they are two or three years old.

Both the siskin and the goldfinch hybridise freely under domestic conditions. Siskins are reasonably early breeders and synchronising their breeding with many other species generally presents few problems. The goldfinch is a little later in coming into breeding condition and under normal conditions should not be expected to fertilise eggs until May. For the breeding of exhibition mules it is usual to pair a siskin or goldfinch cock to a canary hen. However, mules can be produced from the matings in reverse, particularly to produce many of the colour variant mules.

In addition to the canary, the siskin cock has hybridised with the goldfinch, greenfinch, linnet, redpoll and twite, and reverse matings have also been successful. The following rare hybrids, as far as we know, have not yet been authenticated in Great Britain, but are well worth trying:

- Siskin x Bullfinch
- Siskin x Chaffinch
- Siskin x Brambling
- Siskin x Crossbill

In addition to hybridising with the canary the goldfinch cock has hybridised with the siskin, greenfinch, linnet, redpoll and twite, and reverse matings have also been successful. The cock goldfinch has also hybridised with bullfinch and chaffinch hens. Goldfinch x brambling and goldfinch x crossbill hybrids have been authenticated but, as far as we know, have not yet been produced in Great Britain, and are well worth trying.

Hybrids are usually bred in small aviaries or larger cages because they generally require more room than muling pairs. Any hybrids produced can be difficult to rear. Some pairs behave perfectly if supplied with all the natural food we can possibly gather while others, for various reasons, do not rear

Yellow dark siskin mule cock

their young. Bullfinch hens are particularly tricky. In this case you could transfer the eggs to a reliable canary hen and leave her to rear those that hatch on the same diet as that on which she would rear her own young, with the addition of seeding weeds and grasses such as chickweed and dandelion.

When young hybrids leave the nest they should not be removed from their parents until they are eating well for themselves. When weaned they should be provided with the usual seed mixture and egg food, together with soaked seed and all the wild foods which can be gathered, as well as a shallow dish of water in which to bathe. Start colour feeding at about six weeks old. Ready-mixed colour foods and ™Caraphil Red (Roche Products Ltd) can be obtained from most seedsmen and are recommended. Colour feeding should be continued until well after the birds have completed their moult.

You need not ring mules and hybrids, although you can if you wish. Whether ringed or not they can legally be bought, sold and exhibited, provided that both parents are listed on Schedule 3 Part 1 of the Wild Life and Countryside Act 1981. The canary can be one parent provided that the other is on Schedule 3 Part 1. At the time of writing this Act is under review. Hopefully any changes will be beneficial to this side of our hobby.

Exhibition birds should

Gold satinette canary x siskin mule

show clearly the characteristics of both parents and be of good size in regard to the species from which they are bred. They must have good colour. Mules and hybrids, other than some colour variants, are always colour fed for exhibition. They must be of nice cobby type and excel in quality and condition of feather.

Mutations & Colour Variants

It is not the intention of this book to delve too deeply into the world of genetics. However, some basic understanding of the genetic inheritance patterns of colour mutations is necessary if we are to control, improve and generally make the best use of these mutations.

There are three modes of inheritance: dominant, recessive sex-linked and recessive autosomal. If we were to look deeper within each of these groups we would find deviations such as incomplete dominants and full dominants, multiple alleles and deep recessives. If you wish to delve further into the subject you will find that many books have been published about it.

MUTATION INHERITANCE CHARTS

The following charts are for the guidance of those taking up the breeding of colour variants and can be applied to any species. However, they refer only to pairings involving the use of a single mutated colour form with that of pure normal, not to cross-colour pairing expeditions. The latter involve more than one colour form and are covered elsewhere.

Note

In the charts and pairing expectations used throughout, the cock is always listed first in the pairings and the following symbols are used:

/	denotes 'split', carrier of the mutation
-	when between two varieties, refers to a composite variety
SF	denotes single-factor dominant
DF	denotes double-factor dominant
=	denotes progeny expectations

Recessive, Sex-linked Mutation Chart

(referred to as **Sex-linked**)

Normal/Sex-linked   x   Normal   =   Normal Cocks, Normal/Sex-linked Cocks, Normal Hens, Sex-linked Hens

Normal   x   Sex-linked   =   Normal/Sex-linked Cocks, Normal Hens

Normal/sex-linked   x   Sex-linked   =   Normal/Sex-linked Cocks, Sex-linked Cocks, Normal Hens, Sex-linked Hens

Sex-linked   x   Normal   =   Normal/Sex-linked Cocks, Sex-linked Hens

Sex-linked   x   Sex-linked   =   Sex-linked Cocks, Sex-linked Hens

Recessive Autosomal Mutation Chart

(referred to as **Recessive**)

Normal/Recessive   x   Normal   =   Normal Cocks, Normal/Recessive Cocks, Normal Hens, Normal/Recessive Hens

(Reverse pairing gives same expectations)

Normal/Recessive   x   Normal/Recessive   =   Normal Cocks, Normal/Recessive Cocks, Recessive Cocks, Normal Hens, Normal/Recessive Hens, Recessive Hens

Recessive   x   Normal   =   Normal/Recessive Cocks, Normal/Recessive Hens

(Reverse pairing gives same expectations)

Recessive   x   Normal/Recessive   =   Normal/Recessive Cocks, Recessive Cocks, Normal/Recessive Hens, Recessive Hens

(Reverse pairing gives same expectations)

Recessive   x   Recessive   =   Recessive Cocks, Recessive Hens

Dominant Mutation Chart

Dominant (SF)   x   Normal   =   Normal Cocks, Dominant (SF) Cocks, Normal Hens, Dominant (SF) Hens

(Reverse pairing gives same expectations)

Dominant (SF)   x   Dominant (SF)   =   Normal Cocks, Dominant (SF) Cocks, Dominant (DF) Cocks, Normal Hens, Dominant (SF) Hens, Dominant (DF) Hens

Dominant (SF)   x   Dominant (DF)   =   Dominant (SF) Cocks, Dominant (DF) Cocks, Dominant (SF) Hens, Dominant (DF) Hens

(Reverse pairing gives same expectations)

Dominant (DF)   x   Normal   =   Dominant (SF) Cocks, Dominant (SF) Hens

(Reverse pairing gives same expectations)

Dominant (DF)   x   Dominant (DF)   =   Dominant (DF) Cocks, Dominant (DF) Hens

SPONTANEOUS SPORTS

Mutated colour forms appear from time to time through spontaneous sports and, unless these are preserved by correct matings, they can disappear as quickly as they came. Some understanding of genetics will certainly increase our ability to perpetuate mutations through these chance arrivals by enabling us to discover the mode of inheritance. This is secondary to establishing the colour form and follows through from the elimination of inheritance modes one at a time.

Double-factor pastel siskin cock

Dominant Mutations

These are the easiest to establish, since a visual colour form of this mutation is capable of producing its own likeness in the first generation, irrespective of its sex and without any inbreeding.

When you are breeding dominants the colour form is visual and cannot be carried by a normal in hidden form (generally known as a split form). New colour forms that are dominant mutations can turn up as spontaneous sports at any time, male or female, but they are always in what is known as 'single-factor' form, an incomplete dominant. As will be seen from the chart, when one of these is paired to a normal, half of the progeny are of the mutation colour. However, when two single factors of the mutation are paired together they produce young of which 25% are of normal colour and 75% of the mutated colour. Of the mutated young, 25% will receive a double dose of the factor producing the mutation (known as 'double-factor') and they may be visually different (in a dilute factor, much paler) or appear the same. Double-factor forms of the mutation are fully dominant and, when paired to normals, produce all mutation young of the single-factor type. So it will be seen that dominant mutations are not only the easiest to establish but also lend themselves to improvements in exhibition qualities when paired to good exhibition-type normals.

Groundsel

Recessive Sex-linked Mutations

These are not so easy to establish. Although the rules governing sex-linked inheritance are quite straightforward it is important to remember that the results from pairing a sex-linked cock of a mutated colour form to a normal hen are quite different to those obtained from pairing a normal-coloured cock to a sex-linked mutation hen. The reason for this is that a cock can be either pure normal or a visual normal bird with the ability to pass on the colour mutation to some of his young (referred to as a 'carrier' or 'split') or of a visual mutated colour form; whereas a hen can only be a normal-coloured bird or a visual colour mutation. In other words, a normal-coloured hen cannot be split for the sex-linked mutation; she is what you see. Unfortunately there is no significant visual difference between a normal cock and a visual normal cock carrying the mutation factor, so its true genetic make-up can only be proven through test matings. However, as can be seen from the chart on page 53, certain matings produce visual normal cocks guaranteed to be carriers of the mutation.

When a sex-linked colour mutation turns up, the first bird of the mutated form is always a hen. If such a hen is paired to a normal-colour cock all the young produced, both cocks and hens, will be of normal colour, but all the young cocks, although of normal appearance, will carry the new colour. If these young cocks are paired to normal hens 25% of the young produced will be of the mutation colour. Because of the mode of inheritance these will all be hens, and normal hens will also be produced. All the young cocks produced will be visual normals, half of them pure normal

Shepherd's purse

Phaeo-melanistic goldfinch

and the other half carriers of the mutation colour. These young cocks would need to be test-mated to find out which are carrying the mutated gene.

It follows that, to establish the new colour in the shortest possible time, we need to obtain a new-colour cock. To do this we must resort to inbreeding, pairing a new-colour hen to either her father or one of her sons: a practice which should not be taken too far because it can lead to infertility, dead-in-shell or deformed and weak chicks. Once the new-colour cock has been produced it can be paired to an unrelated normal hen. All the young hens of the pairing will then be of the mutated colour and all the young cocks will be of normal appearance but carrying the mutation. These are called 'carriers' or 'splits' and shown as 'normal/mutation' on the tables. When sufficient distantly-related cocks and hens of the new colour are produced they can be paired together to give a clutch in which all the young, cocks and hens, are of the new mutated colour form.

Ragwort

Recessive Autosomal Mutations

Because of their mode of inheritance, these can be difficult to establish. Inbreeding is necessary at first to establish these colour forms, despite the hazards described above. Patience and perseverance are essential to see these colour forms fully established. It is important to remember that unlike the dominants and sex-linked mutations, splits occur in both cocks and hens.

It is also important to realise that the mutation must be present in both parents before visual examples can be produced. Recessive mutations can be carried for many generations in hidden split form but, when two splits come together, the visual form of the mutation will be produced. These can be either cocks or hens. You can then pair these back to the opposite-sex parent. Such a pairing will produce more of the mutation in visual form and all the non-visual young produced will be carriers of the mutation.

This method will achieve results in the shortest possible time but, as already discussed, at the risk of producing weak and sickly mutation young. In the long term it would be better to outcross with the visual mutation by pairing it to one, two or more unrelated normals. This pairing, although not producing any visual forms of the mutation, would produce all young splits for the mutation. You can then pair these more distantly related birds together, split x split, producing much stronger young of the mutated colour form and thus ensuring a better chance of the survival and establishment of the mutation.

SISKIN MUTATIONS

Rare sightings of colour variants have been recorded in wild flocks of both siskin and goldfinch and have cropped up occasionally in domestic stocks but, until recently, none of these rarities had been established successfully. In recent years a few dedicated breeders have made progress, particularly with the siskin, and two mutations of this species are now fully established in Great Britain. Both mutations originated in Belgium, where small stocks had been built up during the 1970s. Most of the work in establishing these mutations in Great Britain was carried out by Fred Fantom of Warley, West Midlands, Bob Partridge, and a few of their close associates. A small importation by Roger Caton in the 1980s further boosted these stocks.

Brown (Dark-eyed Brown)

The first siskin mutation to become established was the brown (dark-eyed brown, see picture on page 21). It is a dark-eyed dilute mutation, sex-linked in its mode of inheritance. In this mutation all melanin pigments are diluted to some degree (approximately 50%). Because hen siskins have very little black melanin in their make-up, the effect of this mutation is to make them appear greyish-brown. Intensive coloured hens appear browner than their non-intensive (buff) counterparts. Since it is sex-linked, the brownish hens of this mutation appeared before the cocks, so one can well understand why early breeders called this mutation 'brown'. However, when the cock of the mutation is produced, we see he is only slightly brown, much of the black melanin remaining, particularly in the cap and primary feathers.

Since the appearance does not easily fit known mutations in other species it will probably go on being called 'brown', possibly with the prefix 'dark-eyed'. However, some breeders believe future experimental pairings will prove the mutation to be very similar, if not identical, to that which gives us the agate in canaries, greenfinches, redpolls and other species. They contend that the distribution of pigments in differing density causes variations within the mutations, giving the same mutation a slightly different appearance in each species.

Mugwort

The following table of pairings shows the expectations, when paired to normal.

Table 1

1	Normal/Brown	x	Normal	=	Normal Cocks, Normal Cocks/Brown, Normal Hens, Brown Hens
2	Normal	x	Brown	=	Normal Cocks/Brown, Normal Hens
3	Normal/Brown	x	Brown	=	Normal Cocks/Brown, Brown Cocks, Normal Hens, Brown Hens
4	Brown	x	Normal	=	Normal Cocks/Brown, Brown Hens
5	Brown	x	Brown	=	Brown Cocks , Brown Hens

Pastel

The second siskin mutation established has become known as the 'pastel'. This is a dominant form of dilute, again a dark-eyed dilute mutation. The diluting factor in this mutation has a different effect on the melanin pigments to that of the previous mutation, although the lipochrome pigment is still unaffected. The mutation is produced in both single- and double-factor forms, and we are fortunate in that it gives two different colour phases to the mutation.

In the single-factor form, the melanin reduction produces a bird that, at first glance, is similar to the dark-eyed brown sex-linked dilute. However, closer examination reveals a greater diluting effect on all the melanin pigments, particularly the eumelanin pigments. This is very noticeable in the wings, where these pigments are almost completely removed from areas of the webbing and give a distinctive laced, or spangled, effect.

In the double-factor form, the melanin is almost completely suppressed, revealing much more of the yellow lipochrome ground

Spearthistle

colour. Although it is a dark-eyed mutation, the strength of the diluting factor in the double factor can give a newly-hatched chick a pink-eyed appearance, the eyes quickly darkening as melanin pigment forms. Some early breeders called this double-factor form the yellow mutation but, to avoid confusion at some future date, it is better to refer to them correctly as double-factor pastels (see page 54).

It will be seen from Table 2 of pairings that their production was relatively simple once stocks became firmly established. It will also be noted that it is only when a double factor is used that the mutation is found to be completely dominant to normal, the single-factor form being only partially dominant. It is essential for colour breeders to experiment by pairing different mutations together to gain knowledge and produce new colour variants. However, from an exhibitor's point of view, to produce examples of the correct colour and purity it is important to keep the different mutations pure. Type and size can be improved or maintained by pairing with good normals.

Table 2

1	Pastel SF	x	Normal	=	Normal Cocks, Pastel Cocks SF, Normal Hens, Pastel Hens SF
	(Reverse Pairing gives same expectations)				
2	Pastel SF	x	Pastel SF	=	Normal Cocks, Pastel Cocks SF, Pastel Cocks DF, Normal Hens, Pastel Hens SF, Pastel Hens DF
3	Pastel DF	x	Normal	=	Pastel Cocks SF, Pastel Hens SF
	(Reverse Pairing gives same expectations)				
4	Pastel SF	x	Pastel DF	=	Pastel Cocks SF, Pastel Cocks DF, Pastel Hens SF, Pastel Hens DF
	(Reverse Pairing gives same expectations)				
5	Pastel DF	x	Pastel DF	=	Pastel Cocks DF, Pastel Hens DF

Brown-Pastel

Brown-pastel is a combination colour already achieved, known as Isabel by some breeders (incorrectly, since Isabel generally refers to a combination of Agate and Cinnamon).

In Table 3 it can be seen that brown-pastels are produced in both single- and double-factor forms. The single-factor form (see page 37) is a pale version of the brown. The double-factor brown-pastel (see page 34) is similar to the double-factor pastel, but has an even clearer yellow with faint brownish markings.

When brown is combined with pastel, brown always behaves as a sex-linked recessive to the pastel, irrespective of whether single- or double-factor forms are used. It will be seen from Table 3 of pairings that brown-pastel hens can only be produced when a visual or split brown male is used. Brown-pastel males are only produced when a brown or split-brown male is paired to a brown female. In other words, Pairings 1, 2 and 4 produce only hens of the brown-pastel single-factor form, Pairing 5 produces both cocks and hens of this colour, and Pairing 6 gives brown-pastel hens in both single-factor and double-factor forms.

Table 3

1	Normal/Brown	x	Pastel SF	=	Normal Cocks, Normal Cocks/Brown, Pastel Cocks SF, Pastel Cocks SF/Brown, Normal Hens, Pastel Hens SF, Brown Hens, Brown-Pastel Hens SF
2	Pastel SF/Brown	x	Normal	=	Normal Cocks, Normal Cocks/Brown, Pastel Cocks SF, Pastel Cocks SF/Brown, Normal Hens, Pastel Hens SF, Brown Hens, Brown Pastel Hens SF
3	Pastel SF	x	Brown	=	Normal Cocks/Brown, Pastel Cocks SF/Brown, Normal Hens, Pastel Hens SF

Silver-agate canary x siskin mule hen

4   Brown   x   Pastel SF = Normal Cocks/Brown, Pastel Cocks SF/Brown, Brown Hens,
                                        Brown-Pastel Hens SF
5   Pastel SF/Brown x   Brown   = Normal Cocks/Brown, Pastel Cocks SF/Brown, Brown Cocks,
                                        Brown-Pastel Cocks SF, Normal Hens, Pastel Hens SF,
                                        Brown Hens, Brown-Pastel Hens SF

6   Pastel SF/Brown x   Pastel SF =   Normal Cocks, Normal Cocks/Brown, Pastel Cocks SF, Pastel Cocks SF/Brown, Pastel Cocks DF, Pastel Cocks DF/Brown, Normal Hens, Brown Hens, Pastel Hens SF, Pastel Hens DF, Brown-Pastel Hens SF, Brown-Pastel Hens DF

In the following tables, Table 4 shows expectations from pairings using single-factor brown-pastels. Table 5 shows what happens when you use double-factor pastels with browns. In Tables 6 and 7 double-factor brown-pastels are used with single-factor pastels, and single-factor to double-factor. In Table 8, double-factor brown-pastels are used with double factor pastels. It can therefore be seen that the two established mutations have provided us with five colour variants: brown, pastel (SF), pastel (DF), brown-pastel (SF) and brown-pastel (DF).

Table 4

1	Normal	x	Brown-Pastel SF	=	Normal Cocks/Brown, Pastel Cocks SF/Brown, Normal Hens, Pastel Hens SF
2	Normal/Brown	x	Brown-Pastel SF	=	Normal Cocks/Brown, Pastel Cocks SF/Brown, Brown Cocks,Brown-Pastel Cocks SF, Normal Hens, Pastel Hens SF, Brown Hens, Brown-Pastel Hens SF
3	Brown-Pastel SF	x	Normal	=	Normal Cocks/Brown, Pastel Cocks SF/Brown, Brown Hens, Brown-Pastel Hens SF
4	Pastel SF	x	Brown-Pastel SF	=	Normal Cocks/Brown, Pastel Cocks SF/Brown, Pastel Cocks DF/Brown, Normal Hens, Pastel Hens SF, Pastel Hens DF
5	Brown-Pastel SF	x	Pastel SF	=	Normal Cocks/Brown, Pastel Cocks SF/Brown, Pastel Cocks DF/Brown, Brown Hens, Brown-Pastel Hens SF, Brown-Pastel Hens DF
6	Pastel SF/Brown	x	Brown-Pastel SF	=	Normal Cocks/Brown, Brown Cocks, Pastel Cocks SF/Brown, Pastel Cocks DF/Brown, Brown-Pastel Cocks SF, Brown-Pastel Cocks DF, Normal Hens, Brown Hens, Pastel Hens SF, Pastel Hens DF, Brown-Pastel Hens SF, Brown-Pastel Hens DF
7	Brown-Pastel SF	x	Brown-Pastel SF	=	Brown-Pastel Cocks SF, Brown-Pastel Cocks DF, Brown-Pastel Hens SF, Brown-Pastel Hens DF

Table 5

1	Normal/Brown	x	Pastel DF	=	Pastel Cocks SF, Pastel Cocks SF/Brown, Pastel Hen SF, Brown-Pastel Hens SF
2	Pastel DF/Brown	x	Normal	=	Pastel Cocks SF, Pastel Cocks SF/Brown, Pastel Hens SF, Brown Pastel Hens SF
3	Pastel DF	x	Brown	=	Pastel Cocks SF/Brown, Pastel Hens SF
4	Brown	x	Pastel DF	=	Pastel Cocks SF/Brown, Brown-Pastel Hens SF
5	Pastel DF/Brown	x	Brown	=	Pastel Cocks SF/Brown, Brown-Pastel Cocks SF, Pastel Hens SF, Brown-Pastel Hens SF
6	Pastel DF/Brown	x	Pastel DF	=	Pastel Cocks DF, Pastel Cocks DF/Brown, Pastel Hens DF, Brown-Pastel Hens DF

Table 6

1	Normal	x	Brown-Pastel DF	=	Pastel Cocks SF/Brown, Pastel Hens SF
2	Normal/Brown	x	Brown-Pastel DF	=	Pastel Cocks SF/Brown, Brown-Pastel Cocks SF, Pastel Hens SF, Brown-Pastel Hens SF
3	Brown-Pastel DF	x	Normal	=	Pastel Cocks SF/Brown, Brown-Pastel Hens SF
4	Pastel SF	x	Brown-Pastel DF	=	Pastel Cocks SF/Brown, Pastel Cocks DF/Brown, Pastel Hens SF, Pastel Hens DF
5	Brown-Pastel DF	x	Pastel SF	=	Pastel Cocks SF/Brown, Pastel Cocks DF/Brown, Brown-Pastel Hens SF, Brown-Pastel Hens DF
6	Pastel SF/Brown	x	Brown-Pastel DF	=	Pastel Cocks SF/Brown, Pastel Cocks DF/Brown, Brown-Pastel Cocks SF, Brown-Pastel Cocks DF, Pastel Hens SF, Pastel Hens DF, Brown-Pastel Hens SF, Brown Pastel Hens DF

Table 7

1	Pastel DF	x	Brown-Pastel SF	=	Pastel Cocks SF/Brown, Pastel Cocks DF/Brown, Pastel Hens SF, Pastel Hens DF
2	Brown-Pastel SF	x	Pastel DF	=	Pastel Cocks SF/Brown, Pastel Cocks DF/Brown, Brown-Pastel Hens SF, Brown-Pastel Hens DF
3	Pastel DF/Brown	x	Brown-Pastel SF	=	Pastel Cocks SF/Brown, Pastel Cocks DF/Brown, Brown-Pastel Cocks SF, Brown-Pastel Cocks DF, Pastel Hens SF, Pastel Hens DF, Brown-Pastel Hens SF, Brown-Pastel Hens DF
4	Brown-Pastel SF	x	Brown-Pastel DF	=	Brown-Pastel Cocks SF, Brown-Pastel Cocks DF, Brown-Pastel Hens SF, Brown-Pastel Hens DF

(Reverse Pairing gives same expectations.)

Table 8

1	Pastel DF	x	Brown-Pastel DF	=	Pastel Cocks DF/Brown, Pastel Hens DF
2	Brown-Pastel DF	x	Pastel DF	=	Pastel Cocks DF/Brown, Brown-Pastel Hens DF
3	Pastel DF/Brown	x	Brown-Pastel DF	=	Pastel Cocks DF/Brown, Brown-Pastel Cocks DF, Pastel Hens DF, Brown-Pastel Hens DF
4	Brown-Pastel DF	x	Brown-Pastel DF	=	Brown-Pastel Cocks DF, Brown-Pastel Hens DF

Other Mutations

Other colour mutations produced in this species to date are cinnamon, lutino and/or satinette, opal and pied, but these have not yet been established. No doubt they will be in due course, giving us a marvellous range of colours for this popular little bird.

GOLDFINCH MUTATIONS

Although a number of colour variant goldfinches have been produced, including albino, white, pied, brown, silver and phaeomelanin, none is as yet established. Most mutations of this species have proved to be recessive autosomal in their mode of inheritance, which can be the most difficult of all mutations to fix and establish. However, in view of the persistence of colour breeders, it is only a matter of time before many of these present rarities become fully established.

Chapter 11

The Law

It is beyond the scope of this volume to give a full explanation of the Wild Life and Countryside Act 1981, which is the current bird protection act; it is both long and complicated. All keepers and breeders of birds, especially keepers and breeders of our native British birds, should make themselves fully acquainted with its provisions. Copies of the Act can be obtained from Her Majesty's Stationery Office. However, some of the most important points are as follows:

1   All wild birds, their nests and eggs are protected.

2   It is illegal to have any wild bird in your possession unless you have a special licence or permit to do so. A bird is only considered to be legally captive-bred if its parents were legally in captivity at the time that it was hatched in a cage or aviary. If you can prove that, the bird need not be ringed; but it is recommended that whenever possible all young birds are ringed.

3   It is illegal to buy or sell a native bird except by special licence unless it is listed only on Schedule 3 Part 1 of the Wild Life and Countryside Act 1981, and then again provided that it is correctly ringed with an approved ring of the correct size. (The siskin and goldfinch are both so listed.)

4   Except under special licence, only birds listed on Schedule 3 Part 1 can be exhibited, and again they must be ringed with an approved ring of the correct size.

5   It is illegal to keep or confine any bird whatsoever in a cage that is not sufficient in height, length or breadth to permit the bird to stretch its wings freely except when:

(a) the bird is in the course of conveyance.

(b) the bird is undergoing treatment by a veterinary surgeon.

(c) the bird is being exhibited for competition. (However, it must not remain in a show cage for more than 72 hours.)

(d) the bird is being trained for exhibition. (However, it must not be so confined for more than one hour in any 24-hour period.)

Tribute

Sadly Peter Lander died before the series *Popular British Birds in Aviculture* could be published.

I first met Peter in the early 1960s when he approached me for some Siberian goldfinches. The goldfinch was a species for which he had a particular fondness.

In addition to keeping and breeding birds, Peter had a keen interest in all things ornithological. I found him a quiet, unassuming man who knew his own mind. He was the driving force behind the founding of The British Bird Council, and worked tirelessly on its behalf for many years. In recent years, by his own choice, he took a back seat, but was always there when needed to give advice and a helping hand.

I worked with Peter when he compiled *British Birds in Aviculture* for the British Bird Council and felt privileged when he asked me to be co-author of the *Popular British Birds in Aviculture* series. Without Peter's initiative this series would not have been produced.

A guiding light extinguished, but memories will light our way.

Bob Partridge